D0759021

to where you came from.
You bug me.
hate you.
You pig.
You are gross.
You're a reject.
You can't do it?
Don't tell anyone.
sucks. Don't you ever
Screw you.
You're crazy
I'm gonna tell
You are worthless.
What are you?
You stink.
Get lost.
Go back
Hey sucker
get you.
see my
watch out
to mommy
You jerk
Wanna fight?
Give me that.
You reek.
like a girl.
Mommy's
You are dumb.
You are a joke.
You scared?
clueless

You are gross. Sucks. Don't you ever wash? You're crazy. You stink. Screw you. You're a reject. You are worthless. Don't you ever wash? You are a joke. I'll are a joke. You're gonna tell back you w I'm gonna tell. Hey sucker. see my Mommy's see mommy. catch out. You came You reek. You're crazy. You're gonna tell. You scared? You can't do it? Get lost. You are worthless. You don't Walk Give me that Don't tell anyone. Mommy's with one You. Get with one eye. What are you? You are worthless. You pig. hate you. to where you came from. jerk. You bug me. You are gross. hate you. Screw you. sucks. Don't you ever wash? You're crazy. You reek. I'm gonna tell with one eye. You pig. You're a reject. Don't tell anyone. hate you. like a girl. You are worth less like a girl. jerk. clueless cry to mommy. drag to get you. Go sucker. You came Mommy's

Wanna fight? Get lost. Go back. What are you? Hey. See my. I'm gonna tell. a dog. see my. Hey. You stink. You reek. catch out. to mommy. get you. see my. Hey. You're. Don't you ever. You're a joke! a dog. a girl. Give me that. You. see my. Hey sucker. Go back. You're crazy. You reek. hate you. What are you? You stink. dumb. out. You are gross. hate you. You bug me. to where you came from. You are worthless. Don't tell anyone. Get. Don't. Screw you. You pig. Mommy's. Get lost. Wanna fight? You stink. You are You are worthless. dumb. out. like a girl.

BULLY 101

written and illustrated by

Doretta Groenendyk

The Acorn Press
Charlottetown
2012

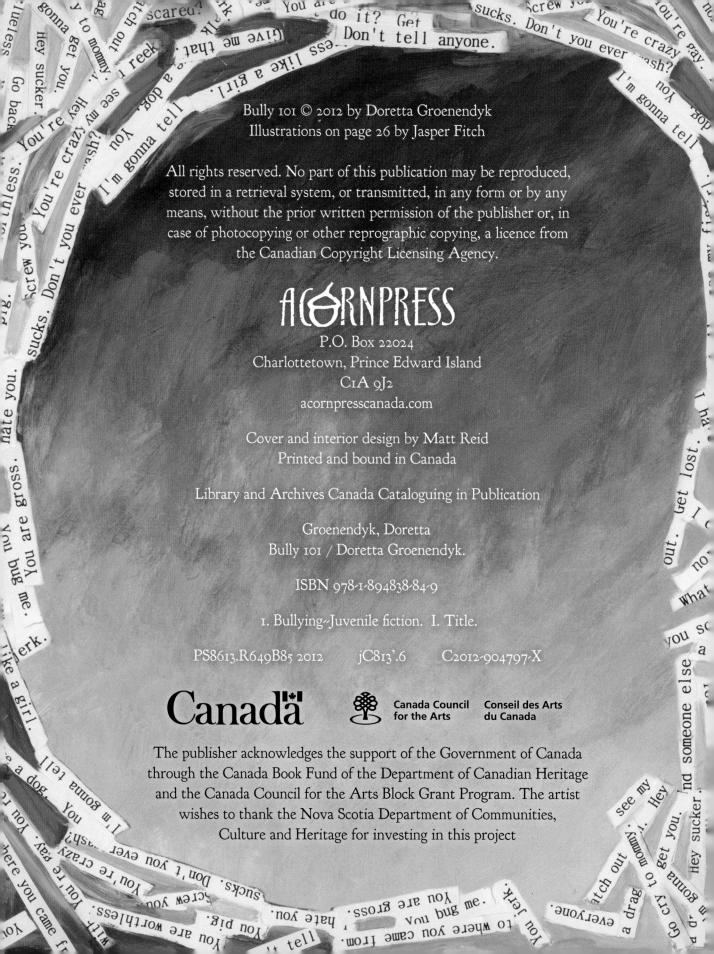

Bully 101 © 2012 by Doretta Groenendyk
Illustrations on page 26 by Jasper Fitch

ACORNPRESS

P.O. Box 22024
Charlottetown, Prince Edward Island
C1A 9J2
acornpresscanada.com

Cover and interior design by Matt Reid
Printed and bound in Canada

Library and Archives Canada Cataloguing in Publication

Groenendyk, Doretta
Bully 101 / Doretta Groenendyk.

ISBN 978-1-894838-84-9

1. Bullying–Juvenile fiction. I. Title.

PS8613.R649B85 2012   jC813'.6   C2012-904797-X

The publisher acknowledges the support of the Government of Canada through the Canada Book Fund of the Department of Canadian Heritage and the Canada Council for the Arts Block Grant Program. The artist wishes to thank the Nova Scotia Department of Communities, Culture and Heritage for investing in this project

for my family, friends and
all those who act in kindness

- Doretta

Welcome to school!
We have a great class,
a real wicked course
you can fight to pass.
If you're feeling low
or a little undone,
blame someone else
in Bully 101.

We'll choose a kid
that's smaller than us
and call her names
while we ride the bus.
If you're kind of down
or a little blue,
steal a kid's notebook
in lesson two.

Give me that.
You're sick.
You are a wimp.
Stupid!
one eye open.
Mommy's boy
You jerk.
Give me that.
clueless.
Hey Ugly.
Get lost.
Go find someone
Sleep
dress like
You are so smart.
like a dog.
anyone
What

Stop talking to that teacher's pet.
We'll make sure he's full of regret.

Want to make yourself feel better?
We'll just ruin that boy's new sweater.

Poke fun of those
who are different or weird.
We'll make sure that we are feared!
We'll laugh at those who make mistakes,
humiliate kids, whatever it takes.

Want to ensure you get your way?
Just mess up another kid's day.

Push them and shove them
and give them a scare.
Our bullies love fear and thrive on a dare.

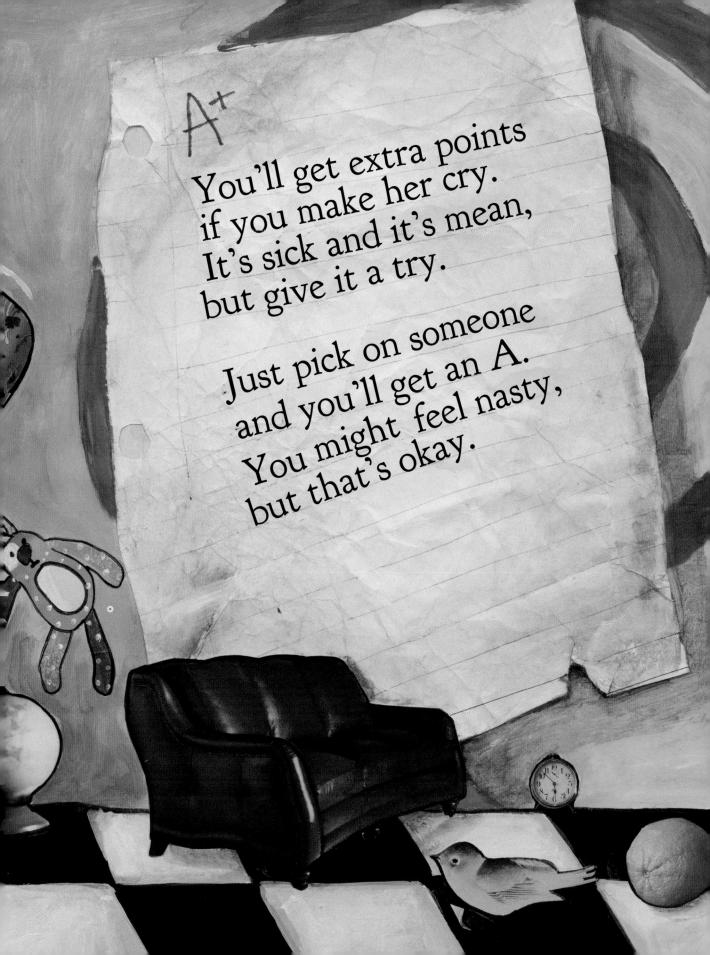

If our bully class
leaves you feeling down
and you prefer peace
to pushing others around,
Bully 101 is not for you.
You might consider Kindness 202.

...rm heartedness gentleness shar
...indness friendship please suppo
...ccomodate help companion serve
...asy going sympathetic celebrate
...nutual link unite include allo
...mbrace forgive tolerate understan
...negotiate peace soothe settle u
...ike   solace
...ood te   mdy
...ide n   take sp
...well wi   ual lis
...ellow   volve u
...artak   ho ey
...selfles   ness an
                                          union
...houghtful cooperate mend heal
...restore improve selfless empathy
...nder charity merciful carry
...nerous connect neighbourly
...harmony nurse encourage cheer
...nurture foster akin walk in
...someone else's shoes connect bond

to where you came from.
You pig.
hate you.
You are gross.
You're a reject.
sucks. Don't you ever wash?
Screw you.
Don't tell anyone.
You can't do it? Get lost.
You are worthless.
You stink.
What are you?
I'm gonna tell
You bug me.
Give me that
You jerk.
You're crazy
Go back
Hey sucker
get you.
see my
Mommy's
Wanna fight?
like a girl.
a dog.
You reek
Watch out
to mommy
You're gay
You are dumb.
You scared
everyone.
drag